COMPARING ANIMAL TRAITS

LEATHERBACK SEA TURTLES
ANCIENT SWIMMING REPTILES

REBECCA E. HIRSCH

Lerner Publications ❖ Minneapolis

Lerner Publications Company
A division of Lerner Publishing Group, Inc.
241 First Avenue North
Minneapolis, MN 55401 USA

For reading levels and more information, look up this title at www.lernerbooks.com.

Photo Acknowledgments

The images in this book are used with the permission of: © Nature Picture Library/Alamy, p. 1; © Wayne Lynch/All Canada Photos/Getty Images, pp. 4, 7 (top), 13, 24, 25 (bottom); © Jurgen Freund/naturepl.com, p. 5; © Visual&WrittenSL/Alamy, p. 6; © Jason Isley/Scubazoo/Getty Images, pp. 7 (bottom), 18; © Matthijs Kuijpers/Alamy, p. 8; © Arco Images GmbH/Alamy, p. 9; © age fotostock Spain S.L./Alamy, p. 10; © NHPA/SuperStock, p. 11 (left); © Janelle Lugge/Shutterstock.com, p. 11 (right); © Laura Westlund/Independent Picture Service, p. 12; © Leonardo Gonzalez/Shutterstock.com, p. 14; © Rick & Nora Bowers/Alamy, p. 16; © National Geographic Image Collection/Alamy, pp. 17, 19 (top); © Frans Lanting Studio/Alamy, p. 19 (bottom); © Michael Patrick O/Neil/Alamy, p. 20 (left); © Adrian Hepworth/Alamy, p. 20 (right); © Pete Oxford/Minden Pictures/Getty Images, pp. 21 (top), 26; © William Mullins/Alamy, p. 21 (bottom); Europics/Newscom, p. 22; © Scubazoo/Alamy, p. 23 (left); © Purestock/Thinkstock, p. 23 (right); © Jim Abernethy/National Geographic/Getty Images, p. 25 (top); © Claus Meyer/Minden Pictures/Getty Images, p. 27 (all); © Jay Ondreicka/Shutterstock.com, p. 28.

Front cover: © Michael Patrick O'Neill/Alamy.
Back cover: Michael Patrick O'Neill/Oceans Image/Photoshot/Newscom.

Main body text set in Calvert MT Std 12/18. Typeface provided by Monotype Typography.

Library of Congress Cataloging-in-Publication Data

Hirsch, Rebecca E., author.
    Leatherback sea turtles : ancient swimming reptiles / Rebecca E. Hirsch.
        pages   cm. — (Comparing animal traits)
    Audience: Ages 7–10.
    Audience: Grades K to 3.
    Includes bibliographical references.
    ISBN 978-1-4677-7980-7 (lb : alk. paper) — ISBN 978-1-4677-8274-6 (pb : alk. paper) —
ISBN 978-1-4677-8275-3 (EB pdf)
    1. Leatherback turtle—Juvenile literature. 2. Sea turtles—Juvenile literature. 3. Leatherback turtle—Behavior—Juvenile literature. 4. Leatherback turtle—Life cycles—Juvenile literature. I. Title.
QL666.C546H57 2015
597.92'89—dc23   2014044315

Manufactured in the United States of America
1 — BP — 7/15/15

TABLE OF CONTENTS

MEET THE LEATHERBACK SEA TURTLE

On a warm summer night, a 1,000-pound (454-kilogram) leatherback sea turtle drags herself out of the water. She pulls her massive body across the sand and looks for a place to dig. Leatherback sea turtles are ancient animals. They have been swimming in the oceans for more than one hundred million years. Leatherback sea turtles belong to a group of animals called reptiles. Other animal groups are insects, fish, amphibians, birds, and mammals.

A female leatherback sea turtle digs her nest.

Reptiles include snakes, lizards, turtles, and crocodiles. Reptiles share many characteristics. All reptiles are vertebrates, meaning they have backbones. Reptiles also have scales on their bodies. All reptiles are cold-blooded, which means that they depend on the temperature of the air or water around them to warm or cool their bodies.

Leatherback sea turtles share these traits with reptiles. But leatherbacks also have traits that make them different from other reptiles.

CHAPTER 1

WHAT DO LEATHERBACK SEA TURTLES LOOK LIKE?

Leatherbacks are the largest turtles in the world. An adult leatherback is usually 4 to 8 feet (1.2 to 2.4 meters) long. The average weight of an adult leatherback sea turtle is between 660 and 1,100 pounds (299 to 499 kg). Larger leatherbacks can weigh more than 2,000 pounds (907 kg). That's nearly as much as a small car!

A leatherback has a black body with white speckles, four flippers, and a shell covered with rubbery skin. Leatherbacks are the only sea turtles with leathery shells. Ridges along the leatherback's carapace (top shell) help give it a streamlined shape so the turtle can move easily through water. A leatherback swims by paddling its front flippers in unison. It steers with its back flippers.

A leatherback sea turtle crawls out of the ocean.

Leatherback sea turtles catch prey in their sharp jaws.

A leatherback has sharp jaws that work like scissors. It uses its jaws to pierce and hold soft foods, such as jellyfish and squid. Spiny barbs line the turtle's mouth and throat. These barbs keep the slippery prey from escaping.

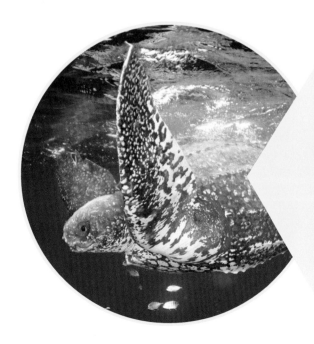

DID YOU KNOW?
The biggest leatherback ever reported was **8.5 FEET** (2.6 m) long and weighed **2,020 POUNDS** (916 kg)!

LEATHERBACK SEA TURTLES VS. PIG-NOSED TURTLES

A pig-nosed turtle paddles underwater. It swims to the surface and takes a breath through its piglike snout. Pig-nosed turtles swim in rivers, lakes, and swamps in Indonesia, Australia, and Papua New Guinea. These freshwater turtles can grow to 29.5 inches (75 centimeters) long and weigh up to 66 pounds (30 kg). As with leatherback sea turtles, pig-nosed turtles have flexible shells covered with leathery skin.

Both leatherback sea turtles and pig-nosed turtles spend most of their lives in the water. Like a leatherback sea turtle, a pig-nosed turtle has a shell that is streamlined for swimming. Its fleshy nose helps it breathe while swimming. When the turtle wants to take a breath, it sticks its nose above the water.

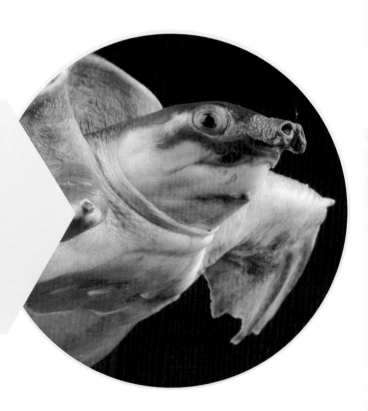

DID YOU KNOW?
All sea turtles have flippers, but the pig-nosed turtle is the only freshwater turtle with **FLIPPERS** instead of feet.

A pig-nosed turtle has long, paddle-shaped flippers. A pig-nosed turtle swims the same way that a leatherback sea turtle does. The pig-nosed turtle rows through the water by moving its front flippers together. It paddles and steers with its back flippers.

A pig-nosed turtle swims using its flippers.

LEATHERBACK SEA TURTLES VS. THORNY DEVILS

A thorny devil stands beside an anthill. Ants run across the ground, and the thorny devil slurps them up with its tongue. Thorny devils are prickly lizards that live in sandy deserts in Australia. Thorny devils are much smaller than leatherbacks. A leatherback sea turtle can grow to more than 8 feet (2.4 m) long. But a thorny devil is only 4 to 6 inches (10 to 15 cm) long. That's shorter than a tube of toothpaste.

A leatherback has flippers and a rubbery shell. But a thorny devil has legs instead of flippers. And instead of a shell, a thorny devil has spiky scales from head to tail. The sharp spikes help protect the thorny devil from predators.

A leatherback sea turtle has traits that make it a good swimmer. But a thorny devil is adapted to the desert. The devil's orange and brown skin color camouflages it against the sand. Grooves on the thorny devil's body help it get a drink in the dry desert. Dew drops collect in grooves between the lizard's spikes. Water runs down the grooves into the thorny devil's mouth.

COMPARE IT!

VS.

LEATHERBACK SEA TURTLES

THORNY DEVILS

	HEAD AND BODY LENGTH	
4 TO 8 FEET (1.2 TO 2.4 M)		**4 TO 6 INCHES** (10 TO 15 CM)

	WEIGHT	
500 TO ABOUT 2,000 POUNDS (227 TO 907 KG)		**1 TO 2 OUNCES** (28 TO 57 GRAMS)

BODY FEATURE

Streamlined shell

Spiky scales

CHAPTER 2

WHERE LEATHERBACK SEA TURTLES LIVE

Leatherbacks swim through oceans around the world. They inhabit tropical and temperate waters. They also swim in chilly waters between 30 and 40°F (−1 and 4°C). Leatherbacks inhabit more places in the world than any other reptile. Leatherbacks have been spotted as far north as Alaska and as far south as South Africa.

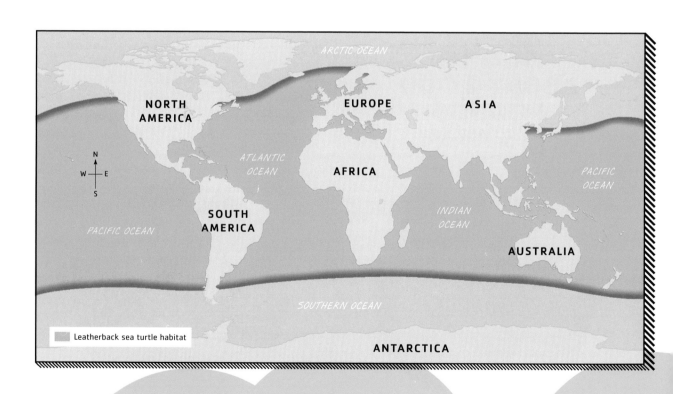

Leatherback sea turtle habitat

DID YOU KNOW?
The longest recorded leatherback migration was nearly **13,000 MILES** (20,921 kilometers).

Leatherbacks don't stay in one place. They wander the open ocean and feast on jellyfish. Every few years, they migrate thousands of miles to waters near warm, sandy nesting beaches. In the water far from shore, males and females mate. Then females crawl onto land to lay their eggs.

Over many years, people have changed leatherback habitats. These changes are dangerous for leatherbacks. In the ocean, leatherbacks sometimes mistake floating plastic trash for jellyfish. Leatherbacks can choke on this garbage. They may get tangled in fishing gear and drown. People build houses on nesting beaches, which also harms turtles. Because of these habitat changes, leatherbacks are in danger of extinction. Scientists estimate that there are between 20,000 and 30,000 adult females compared to 115,000 about thirty years earlier. People must make leatherback habitats safer if this ancient species is to survive.

LEATHERBACK SEA TURTLES VS. LOGGERHEAD SEA TURTLES

A loggerhead turtle glides through a coral reef. Loggerheads are another type of sea turtle. There are seven different species of sea turtles. They come in different shapes and sizes. But they all have streamlined bodies for swimming long distances in the ocean.

Like leatherbacks, loggerhead sea turtles swim in oceans around the world. But loggerheads don't like cold waters the way leatherbacks do. Loggerheads swim close to coasts in the warmer waters of the Atlantic, Pacific, and Indian Oceans. Loggerheads love coral reefs, rocky places, and even shipwrecks, where they find plenty of prey. Like leatherbacks, loggerheads are carnivores. They dive to the ocean bottom and use their powerful jaws to crack open shellfish, clams, and crabs.

Loggerheads migrate to different habitats, as leatherbacks do. Every few years loggerheads travel from their feeding

A loggerhead sea turtle swims near a coral reef on the ocean floor.

COMPARE IT!

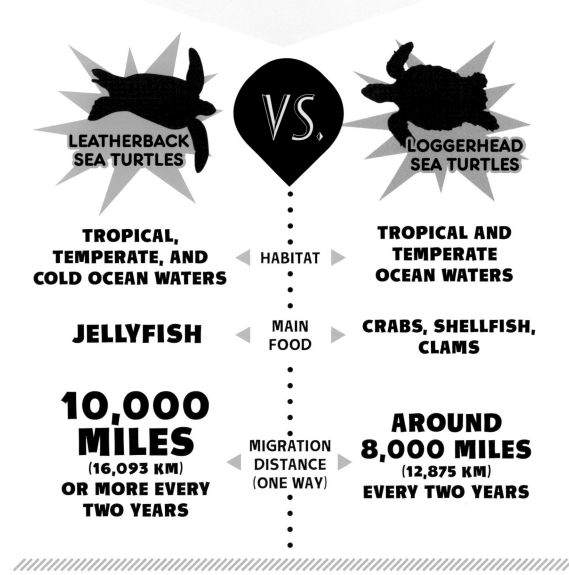

LEATHERBACK SEA TURTLES		LOGGERHEAD SEA TURTLES
TROPICAL, TEMPERATE, AND COLD OCEAN WATERS	◄ HABITAT ►	TROPICAL AND TEMPERATE OCEAN WATERS
JELLYFISH	◄ MAIN FOOD ►	CRABS, SHELLFISH, CLAMS
10,000 MILES (16,093 KM) OR MORE EVERY TWO YEARS	◄ MIGRATION DISTANCE (ONE WAY) ►	AROUND 8,000 MILES (12,875 KM) EVERY TWO YEARS

grounds and swim long distances to reach nesting beaches. Males and females mate in the water, and females lay their eggs on the beach.

Loggerheads face the same threats as leatherbacks. Both species are harmed by fishing gear, plastic trash, and the destruction of nesting beaches. As with leatherbacks, loggerheads are at risk of extinction because of these habitat changes.

LEATHERBACK SEA TURTLES VS. GILA MONSTERS

A Gila (HEE-luh) monster climbs onto a rock and flicks its forked tongue. Gila monsters live in different habitats than leatherback sea turtles. Leatherbacks swim in oceans. Gila monsters inhabit hot, rocky deserts in North America.

Gila monsters live on rocky slopes and in canyons and washed-out gullies. They hunt for lizards, birds, and bird eggs. Gila monsters hunt in the morning and in the late afternoon, when the weather is cooler. During the hottest part of the day, they take shelter in burrows dug in the ground or under rocks and bushes. These shady places help the lizards keep their bodies cool during hot desert days.

A Gila monster eats a bird egg.

Leatherbacks are world travelers. They migrate enormous distances through oceans. But Gila monsters like to stay in one place. A Gila monster uses the same burrow year after year and spends more than 95 percent of its time underground. This reptile comes out only to warm itself in the sun or to hunt nearby for food.

A Gila monster peeks out of its underground burrow.

CHAPTER 3

SWIMMING WITH LEATHERBACK SEA TURTLES

Leatherback sea turtles are powerful swimmers. A leatherback swims alone, moving its long front flippers together in graceful strokes. It looks as if the turtle is flying underwater. Leatherbacks are deep divers. A leatherback can dive as deep as 4,200 feet (1,280 m). Before diving, a leatherback takes a big breath. One breath can last for more than an hour.

Leatherbacks swim in chilly waters filled with jellyfish. But leatherbacks are cold-blooded, like all reptiles. Cold-blooded animals rely on the air or water temperature around them to warm or cool their bodies. So how do leatherbacks stay warm

A leatherback sea turtle dives deep under the sea.

DID YOU KNOW?
Leatherbacks are the fastest swimming reptiles. A leatherback was once clocked swimming at **21.92 MILES** (35.28 km) per hour.

in very cold waters? One way is by swimming constantly. Animals burn energy when they use their muscles. This creates heat. A leatherback can also shut off blood flow to its flippers. That blood then goes to the rest of the leatherback's body. The flippers get cold, but the rest of the body stays warm for longer. Thick layers of fat and a leatherback's large size help keep it warm too. A large body retains heat better than a small one.

Leatherbacks eat salty jellyfish and drink seawater. They need a way to get rid of the excess salt in their bodies. A leatherback has a salt gland in its head that empties into its eyes. The turtle cries the excess salt out through its tears.

Leatherback sea turtles release excess salt through their tears.

LEATHERBACK SEA TURTLES VS. YELLOW-BELLIED SEA SNAKES

A yellow-bellied sea snake swims through ocean currents. Yellow-bellied sea snakes live in the warm waters of the Indian and Pacific Oceans. Leatherback sea turtles and yellow-bellied sea snakes are adapted to ocean life in similar ways.

Both leatherback sea turtles and yellow-bellied sea snakes are powerful swimmers. A leatherback paddles with its flippers. A sea snake glides through the water and uses its flat tail as a paddle. Like leatherbacks, yellow-bellied sea snakes can stay underwater for a long time. These snakes can even breathe underwater through their skin. They can't stay underwater permanently, but the extra oxygen helps them stay under for up to three and a half hours! As with leatherbacks, the snakes still need to rise to the surface to take a deep breath.

While yellow-bellied sea snakes (*right*) use their tail to swim, leatherback sea turtles (*left*) use their flippers.

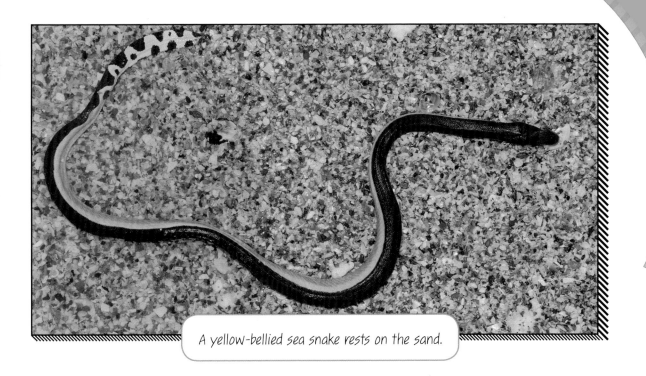

A yellow-bellied sea snake rests on the sand.

The yellow-bellied sea snake eats salty fish and swallows seawater while catching fish. Both leatherback sea turtles and yellow-bellied sea snakes have ways of getting rid of excess salt. The sea snake's salt gland lies under its tongue. The snake flicks its tongue to get rid of excess salt.

DID YOU KNOW?
Yellow-bellied sea snakes do not drink pure seawater. They drink from a thin layer of **FRESHWATER** that collects on top of the ocean after a rain.

LEATHERBACK SEA TURTLES VS. MONKEY-TAILED SKINKS

A monkey-tailed skink slowly climbs a tree on the Solomon Islands in the Pacific Ocean. This green, scaly reptile can grow to 32 inches (81 cm) long. Monkey-tailed skinks not only look different from leatherback sea turtles. They have different behaviors too.

Leatherbacks are solitary. But monkey-tailed skinks are social. They live in groups of up to ten skinks. Leatherbacks swim and dive. Monkey-tailed skinks climb trees. Skinks climb with their sharp claws and use their long, flexible tails to grip branches. Wrapping their tails around branches makes climbing easier and safer.

A leatherback swims fast. But monkey-tailed skinks move very slowly. This helps protect them from predators. The green skink blends in with its surroundings and moves so slowly that predators may not notice it.

A monkey-tailed skink greets its mate.

COMPARE IT!

LEATHERBACK SEA TURTLES VS. **MONKEY-TAILED SKINKS**

| LIVES ALONE | ◀ BEHAVIOR ▶ | **LIVES IN GROUPS** |

| | ◀ HOW IT GETS AROUND ▶ | |

SWIMS AND DIVES | | **CLIMBS TREES**

| **FAST** | ◀ MOVEMENT SPEED ▶ | **SLOW** |

CHAPTER 4
THE LIFE CYCLE OF LEATHERBACK SEA TURTLES

A giant leatherback sea turtle begins life inside an egg about the size of a Ping-Pong ball. After mating, a female leatherback crawls onto a sandy beach, digs a hole, and lays between 60 and 120 eggs—called a clutch. She carefully covers the hole and crawls back to the sea. For the next few weeks, she returns to the beach and lays five to seven clutches. Each clutch is laid in a different hole. Then she leaves the beach and swims away.

The baby turtles grow inside the eggs for about two months. The temperature of the nest determines the sex of the turtles. A warmer nest produces more females. A cooler nest produces more males. The baby turtles inherit traits from their parents. These include long flippers and leathery shells.

A baby leatherback sea turtle crawls from its egg after hatching.

Like their parents, baby turtles have long flippers.

After hatching, the baby turtles dig their way to the surface and race to the water. Life is dangerous for a baby leatherback. Hungry crabs, birds, and sharks snatch the tiny hatchlings on land and in the water. Only about 1 in 1,000 baby turtles will survive to adulthood. If it survives, the baby turtle will grow to its adult size between the ages of seven and thirteen. Turtles that make it to adulthood may live for thirty to fifty years or more.

DID YOU KNOW?
An adult female leatherback often returns to lay her eggs on the **SAME** beach where she was born.

LEATHERBACK SEA TURTLES VS. GIANT SOUTH AMERICAN TURTLES

A giant South American turtle paddles through a muddy river. This freshwater turtle can weigh up to 200 pounds (91 kg) as an adult. It inhabits rivers and ponds in South America. Giant South American turtles and leatherback sea turtles have similar life cycles.

Like leatherbacks, giant South American turtles migrate to their nesting spots. South American turtles migrate from forested riverbanks to sandy riverbanks, where the females lay their eggs. Males and females mate in the water, and females lay their eggs in the sand. Each female digs a hole and lays 61 to 172 eggs, or one to two clutches. The eggs hatch in about two months.

As with leatherbacks, nest temperature controls the sex of giant South American turtle hatchlings. Warm temperatures produce more females. Cool temperatures produce more males. Newly hatched giant South American turtles inherit traits from their parents, such as domed shells and long necks. These turtles may survive for twenty years or more in the wild. This is about half the life span of leatherback sea turtles.

A baby giant South American turtle climbs out of its egg.

LEATHERBACK SEA TURTLES VS. GARTER SNAKES

A garter snake slips through tall grass. Garter snakes live in meadows, marshes, woodlands, and hillsides across North America. They are also commonly found in gardens and backyards. This striped snake can reach 4.5 feet (1.4 m) long, although most garter snakes are smaller. A garter snake looks different from a leatherback sea turtle. It has a different life cycle too.

Leatherback sea turtles hatch from eggs. But garter snakes don't lay eggs. Two to three months after mating, a female garter snake gives birth to about ten to forty babies. Each baby snake is born inside a transparent sac and must slither its way out. The baby snakes are 4.7 to 9 inches (12 to 23 cm) long and look a lot like their parents.

A garter snake rests along a rocky hillside in North America.

COMPARE IT!

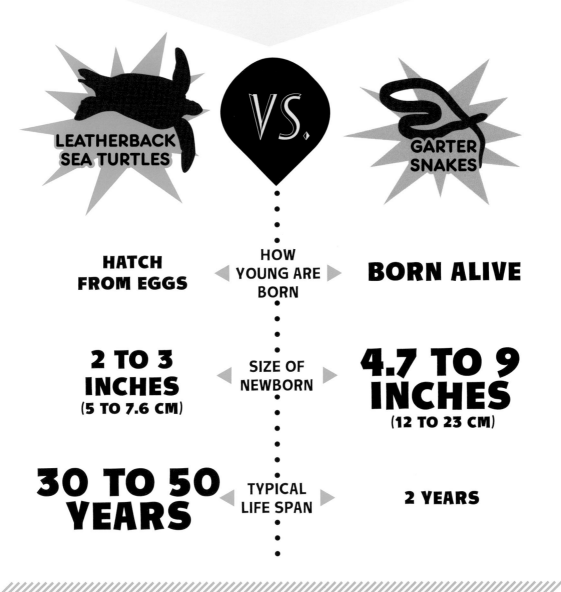

LEATHERBACK SEA TURTLES		GARTER SNAKES
HATCH FROM EGGS	HOW YOUNG ARE BORN	BORN ALIVE
2 TO 3 INCHES (5 TO 7.6 CM)	SIZE OF NEWBORN	4.7 TO 9 INCHES (12 TO 23 CM)
30 TO 50 YEARS	TYPICAL LIFE SPAN	2 YEARS

Once leatherbacks reach adulthood, they may live for up to fifty years. But garter snakes reach adulthood around the age of two and live for only a couple of years in the wild. Garter snakes are prey to many animals, so their life span is much shorter than a leatherback sea turtle's.

LEATHERBACK SEA TURTLES TRAIT CHART

This book introduces leatherback sea turtles and explores some of the ways they are similar to and different from other reptiles. What reptiles would you add to this list?

	COLD-BLOODED	SCALES ON BODY	LAYS EGGS	LEATHERY SHELL	AT RISK OF EXTINCTION	SALT GLANDS
LEATHERBACK SEA TURTLE	X	X	X	X	X	X
PIG-NOSED TURTLE	X	X	X	X		
THORNY DEVIL	X	X	X			
LOGGERHEAD SEA TURTLE	X	X	X		X	X
GILA MONSTER	X	X	X			
YELLOW-BELLIED SEA SNAKE	X	X				X
MONKEY-TAILED SKINK	X	X				
GIANT SOUTH AMERICAN TURTLE	X	X	X			
GARTER SNAKE	X	X				

GLOSSARY

adapted: suited to living in a particular environment

camouflages: makes it possible to blend into an environment with the use of colors or patterns

carapace: a hard shell on the back of some animals, such as turtles or crabs

carnivores: meat-eating animals

clutch: a nest of eggs

excess: an amount that is more than usual or necessary

extinction: the state of no longer existing

habitats: environments where animals naturally live. A habitat is the place where an animal can find food, water, air, shelter, and a place to raise its young.

hatchlings: recently hatched animals

migrate: to move from one place to another for feeding or breeding

predators: animals that hunt, or prey on, other animals

prey: an animal that is hunted and killed by a predator for food

social: living in groups or communities

solitary: living alone

streamlined: smoothly shaped so that moving through water is easier

temperate: a climate that is mild, without extremely cold or extremely hot temperatures

traits: features that are inherited from parents. Body size and skin color are examples of inherited traits.

transparent: see-through

LERNER

Expand learning beyond the printed book. Download free, complementary educational resources for this book from our website, www.lerneresource.com.

SOURCE

SELECTED BIBLIOGRAPHY

Franklin, Carl J. *Turtles: An Extraordinary Natural History 245 Million Years in the Making*. St. Paul: Voyageur Press, 2007.

Halliday, Tim, and Kraig Adler. *Firefly Encyclopedia of Reptiles and Amphibians*. Toronto: Firefly Books, 2002.

"Leatherback Sea Turtle (*Dermochelys coriacea*)." US Fish and Wildlife Service. Accessed October 27, 2014. http://www.fws.gov/northflorida/seaturtles/turtle%20factsheets/leatherback-sea-turtle.htm.

"Leatherback Turtle (*Dermochelys coriacea*)." IUCN SSC Marine Turtle Specialist Group. Accessed October 20, 2014. http://iucn-mtsg.org/about-turtles/species/leatherback/.

"Leatherback Turtle (*Dermochelys coriacea*)." NOAA Fisheries. Last modified June 23, 2014. http://www.nmfs.noaa.gov/pr/species/turtles/leatherback.htm.

"The Leatherback Sea Turtle." National Park Service. Accessed October 17, 2014. http://www.nps.gov/caha/naturescience/leatherbackseaturtle.htm.

FURTHER INFORMATION

Fleisher, Paul. *Ocean Food Webs in Action*. Minneapolis: Lerner Publications, 2014. Discover more about ocean animals and read about ocean food webs in action.

National Geographic: Swimming Machine http://ngm.nationalgeographic.com/2009/05/leatherback-turtles/swimming-machine-interactive Check out this interactive diagram to learn more about how leatherbacks are adapted for deep diving.

Newman, Patricia. *Plastic, Ahoy!: Investigating the Great Pacific Garbage Patch*. Minneapolis: Millbrook Press, 2014. Follow along as a team of scientists studies a danger to sea turtles: plastic trash in the ocean.

NOAA—*The Kid's Times*—Leatherback Sea Turtle http://www.nmfs.noaa.gov/pr/pdfs/education/kids_times_turtle_leatherback.pdf Discover fascinating facts about leatherbacks and how you can help them.

Swinburne, Stephen R. *Sea Turtle Scientist*. Boston: Houghton Mifflin Harcourt, 2014. Learn more about leatherbacks, how they came to be endangered, and what scientists are doing to save them.

INDEX